Design and layout copyright © The Random Century Group 1992
Photographs copyright © Linda Burgess 1992

Published by Clarkson N. Potter, Inc., 201 East 50th Street, New York, NY 10022 Member of the Crown Publishing Group.

Published in Great Britain by Ebury Press in 1992

CLARKSON N. POTTER, POTTER and colophon are trademarks of Clarkson N. Potter, Inc.

Manufactured in Italy

Editor: Jane Struthers
Designer: Polly Dawes

ISBN 0-517-59157-X

Library of Congress cataloguing-in-publication data is available on request.

Typeset by Textype Typesetters, Cambridge
Printed and bound in Italy by New Interlitho S.p.a., Milan

10 9 8 7 6 5 4 3 2 1

Contents

Introduction

Flowers are a constant source of inspiration to me and an essential part of my life. They have inspired painters and poets throughout the ages with their sweet beauty, simplicity and fragrance. Flowers give us universal pleasure, and their constant appeal inspires us to include them in every area of our lives, from clothing, furnishings, ceramics and jewellery to food and celebrations. We use flowers to mark the rituals, changes and events in our lives, such as births, weddings, love, sadness, peace and war, for they symbolize something greater than ourselves.

Throughout this book you will see how I have arranged flowers to bring out their beauty, colour and shape, and also to conjure up distinct moods and atmospheres. I hope my photographs will inspire you to see flowers in a new way, and perhaps even lead you to discover some unusual treasures of the flower world, but above all I hope my pictures will show you the intense pleasure that flowers can give.

LINDA BURGESS

LONDON 1992

Simplicity

NO SPRING, NOR SUMMER BEAUTY HATH SUCH GRACE,

AS I HAVE SEEN IN ONE AUTUMNAL FACE.

from *The Autumnal*, John Donne

PREVIOUS PAGES THIS IS A SIMPLE
COMPOSITION OF WHITE
RHODODENDRON FLOWERS AND SOME
MUCH TREASURED BIRDS' NESTS. YOU
CAN HIDE THE SMALL VASES
CONTAINING THE FLOWERS BY
CAREFULLY POSITIONING THE NESTS
IN FRONT OF THEM. THESE NESTS
HAD BEEN DISCARDED WHEN I
FOUND THEM, BUT PLEASE NEVER
TAKE NESTS FROM HEDGES OR TREES.

RIGHT I LOVE THE IDEA OF
BASKETS OF FLOWERS, AND THESE
WHITE AND PINK RHODODENDRONS
LOOK PRETTY TRAILING OVER THE
SIDE OF A SIMPLE RUSTIC SHOPPING
BASKET. IT DOESN'T MATTER WHAT
SORT OF CONTAINER YOU USE TO
HOLD THE FLOWERS BECAUSE IT
WON'T BE VISIBLE, SO SHORT SQUAT
JAM JARS CAN BE IDEAL. CHANGE
THE WATER EVERY DAY TO PROLONG
THE LIFE OF THE FLOWERS.

FACING PAGE HERE IS A SELECTION
OF VARIOUS RHODODENDRON
FLOWERS. I HAVE GIVEN
EACH VARIETY ITS OWN
CONTAINER AND THEN GROUPED
THEM ALL TOGETHER. CHOOSING
CONTAINERS OF DIFFERENT SIZES
AND SHAPES HELPS TO CREATE
INTEREST AND SHOWS OFF THE
FLOWERS AT THEIR VERY BEST.

SIMPLE ideas can lead to stunning arrangements. You do not need to worry about complicated structures, making the flowers follow certain lines whether they want to or not or feel that anything simple will not be interesting or sophisticated. Forget about those tortured concoctions which looked at home in hairdressers' windows during the Fifties and have been out of place ever since. The poor flowers always look uncomfortable and rigid, and anything but natural. That's what happens when we impose ourselves upon flowers, for the results are so often pinched and tight, but when we let flowers speak for themselves they look delightfully fresh.

Fluid lines and an uncluttered approach are the best ways to create simple arrangements and if you follow these rules you will be able to use an astonish-

BEARDED IRISES BENEFIT FROM HAVING THEIR STEMS TRIMMED BEFORE ARRANGING, AND YOU SHOULD ALSO REMOVE ANY FADED FLOWER HEADS THAT MIGHT DETRACT FROM THE BEAUTY OF THE IRISES. A SELECTION OF VASES (PREFERABLY GLASS) OF VARYING HEIGHTS, AS I HAVE USED HERE, WILL SHOW IRISES OFF TO PERFECTION AS IT CREATES TIERS OF FLOWERS AND THE FLOWER HEADS FUSE TOGETHER TO FORM A CLOUD. FILLING A WHOLE AREA LIKE THIS WITH A SINGLE TYPE OF FLOWER INCREASES THE IMPACT OF THE ARRANGEMENT.

ing array of flowers. Try not to fall into the trap of mentally dividing flowers into different compartments, such as simple or sophisticated, and then never breaking your self-imposed rules. As you look through this book you will find many flowers appearing in more than one chapter, proving that it is often the way you treat the flower that determines its mood.

SIMPLICITY is not a byword for plainness. Rather, it can mean classic flowers that are presented and arranged in uncomplicated ways. The containers on the facing page house a variety of bearded irises. Some are arranged neatly in vases and glasses while others have had their stems cut off and just the heads placed in low bowls. This is a very good way to display irises, or any other garden flowers for that matter, that have broken stems and would not fit in an ordinary vase. The gentle mixture of colours is enlivening and shows once again that there are few rules about matching the colours of flowers.

Irises have been grown by interested gardeners since the sixteenth century, and the bearded varieties are among the most popular. They first appeared in the seventeenth century, when they were a feature of many European gardens and were frequently raised from seed by keen gardeners eager to increase their stock. Iris breeding had become big business in Europe by the 1890s, and America followed suit a decade later. Gertrude Jekyll, one of the most famous garden-

Come into the garden, Maud,
For the black bat, night, has flown;
Come into the garden, Maud,
I am here at the gate alone;
And the woodbine spices are wafted
abroad,
And the musk of the rose is blown.

There has fallen a splendid tear
    From the passion-flower at the gate.
She is coming, my dove, my dear;
She is coming, my life, my fate;
The red rose cries, 'She is near, she
is near;'
    And the white rose weeps, 'She is
    late;'
The larkspur listens, 'I hear, I hear;'
    And the lily whispers, 'I wait.'

from Maud, Alfred, Lord Tennyson

THE END OF SUMMER IS SUGGESTED
BY A BRANCH OF A DECORATIVE
CRAB APPLE (MALUS 'NEVILLE
COPEMAN') AND A LATE BLOOM OF
THE PASSION FLOWER (PASSIFLORA
CAERULEA). THIS IS A TENDER
VINE, THE DISTINCTIVE FLOWERS OF
WHICH HAVE TEN PETALS, A
CORONA AND A CENTRAL STALK
BEARING THE STAMENS AND
OVARY. IT WAS APPARENTLY GIVEN
ITS NAME BECAUSE ITS MARKINGS
ARE SAID TO RESEMBLE THE
WOUNDS OF CHRIST.

ers of the early twentieth century, was particularly fond of irises and even designed gardens especially for them.

G ROWN for four centuries in English gardens and popular in Victorian times, the old-fashioned *Primula auricula* is once again enjoying a well-deserved revival. This species has been cultivated to produce many beautiful, old, dusty colours, including amazing greys, greens, yellows, pinks and reds. My favourite ones are the muted maroon and yellow varieties which remind me of plums and custard. Double auriculas are also grown and look like tiny decorative cabbages. Striped auriculas were tremendously popular in the seventeenth century but have since apparently vanished completely from cultivation. Many auriculas have a sweet and delicate scent that adds to the simple beauty of these lovely flowers.

John Gerard, the sixteenth-century botanist, described snake's head fritillaries (*Fritillaria meleagris*) as being 'greatly esteemed for the beautifying of our gardens and the bosoms of the beautifull'. These wonderful flowers are natives of Britain, but strangely enough that wasn't known until many of the bulbs had been imported back into the country from France in the late 1500s. They were called the 'chequered daffodill' and are still greatly prized for the beautiful chequerboard markings on their petals. Fritillaries are very easy to grow, and if they like their surroundings

Auriculas can be found growing in the Alps, so require a light, gritty alkaline soil. Some types of auricula need full sun while others prefer partial shade, so carefully check the needs of a particular variety before planting it in the garden.

SIMPLICITY

AN UNUSUAL PERSPECTIVE GIVES
ORIENTAL APPEAL TO THIS SINGLE
ARUM LILY (*ZANTEDESCHIA*). IT IS
THE STRIKING COMBINATION OF
YELLOW AND BLACK, WITH THE
PLEASINGLY CURVED LINES OF THE
VASE, WHICH ALLOWS THE GRAPHIC
SIMPLICITY OF THE FLOWER TO
SHINE THROUGH. USING CONTRASTS
IS AN EASY WAY TO ACHIEVE A
SIMPLE ARRANGEMENT, AS IS USING
A SINGLE FLOWER. AN
ARRANGEMENT LIKE THIS IS BEST
VIEWED FROM ABOVE, SO WOULD
LOOK GOOD PLACED ON
A LOW TABLE.

THE FALLEN PETALS OF THE ICELAND POPPY, *PAPAVER NUDICAULE*, MAKE SPLASHES OF COLOUR LIKE CRUSHED TISSUE PAPER. YOU CAN CAPTURE THE LAST PLEASURE OF YOUR FLOWERS BY GATHERING UP THEIR PETALS AND PUTTING THEM IN GLASSES.

in the garden will happily start to multiply and spread in all directions.

ONE of the best ways to brighten up a dull patch of garden border is to sprinkle a packet of poppy seeds over it in spring and then wait for the magic to begin. That area will be ablaze with colour in early summer. It doesn't seem to matter much whether the plants are perennials, biennials or annuals, as their falling seeds are always eager to sow themselves around the garden and appear in all sorts of unlikely places over the years to come. Any seedlings you don't want can simply be pulled out by

OLD GREEN GLASS BOTTLES ARE THE PERFECT CONTAINERS FOR THESE ORIENTAL POPPIES (*PAPAVER ORIENTALE*). MERCIFULLY, YOU CAN PICK THEM FROM THE GARDEN WITH A CLEAR CONSCIENCE WHEN DARK CLOUDS THREATEN A SUMMER'S DAY. INDOORS IS THEN A MUCH SAFER PLACE FOR THEM THAN OUTDOORS, WHERE THEY RISK BEING BATTERED BY HAIL OR HEAVY RAIN DROPS, WHICH COULD PREMATURELY END THEIR BRIEF LIVES. POPPIES ARE QUITE SPOILED WHEN RAIN-SPLATTERED AND LOOK LIKE LITTLE GIRLS WHO HAVE HAD THE MISFORTUNE TO FALL INTO PUDDLES.

❧ ❧ ❧

But pleasures are like poppies spread,
You seize the flower, its bloom is shed.

Tam O'Shanter, Robert Burns

the roots, while the others can be enjoyed for their vivacity and vibrant colours. Pick a dried poppy seed head and shake it, and you'll find you're holding a miniature musical instrument, like a tiny maraca. Empty the seed pod into your palm and you'll be astonished at how many seeds fall out. No wonder poppies are such prolific seeders!

There are many varieties of poppy available, including the sturdy oriental poppy (*Papaver orientale*), with its glaucous green fuzzy leaves and brilliantly enamelled red and black petals, the opium poppies (*P. somniferum*), some of which are double-flowered like floppy carnations, and the papery field poppies (*P. rhoeas*). It is interesting to note how many legends and stories are linked to these plants: the Roman corn goddess Ceres wore a crown of wheat and held a lighted torch in one hand and a bunch of corn and poppies in the other. The poppy was also one of the flowers belonging to Aphrodite, the Greek goddess of vegetation. The opium poppy is said to have sprung up in the place where Buddha cut off his eyelids in order to stay awake, while the field poppy is irrevocably linked with the Flanders fields of the First World War.

The poppies shown on pages 18 and 19 are Iceland poppies (*P. nudicaule*). They are much more delicate than their cousins, the oriental and opium poppies, and look as though the slightest puff of wind will rob them of all their petals. However, they were first

PREVIOUS PAGES THIS IS A REFRESHINGLY SIMPLE WAY TO ARRANGE TULIPS AND IT ALLOWS THEM SOME MOVEMENT WITHIN THE CONFINES OF THEIR VASE. CUT THE STEMS TO DIFFERENT LENGTHS AND THEN PLACE THEM, WITH THE SHORTEST FLOWERS AT THE FRONT AND SIDES, IN A FAN-LIKE ARCH. AS THE FLOWERS CONTINUE TO GROW IN THE WATER YOU WILL BE ABLE TO WATCH THEIR HEADS ENLARGE TO CREATE AN EVEN MORE COLOURFUL IMPACT. LET SOME OF THE TULIPS FLOP OVER THE SIDES OF THE VASE TO RELIEVE ITS HARSH LINES.

found growing, in the early eighteenth century, in Siberia and northern Canada, so are really quite hardy. They are perennials but are best treated as annuals, and are such a pleasure to look at that most gardeners would rather have too many of them than not enough. A profusion of the poppies will also mean some can be spared for cutting, which should be done just before the bud is ready to open either in the early morning or late evening.

The oriental poppy was discovered in 1702 and swiftly taken to France to show Louis XIV. He wasn't the only one to enjoy it, for by the 1740s the seeds were being sent by Quaker seedsmen from London to Philadelphia. Anyone who has grown this lovely plant will join in singing its praises, and will have watched it come into flower with eager anticipation, then no doubt despaired as it has suddenly flopped and lost all its petals, leaving a huge gap in the border. Gertrude Jekyll's solution to this problem was to fill the gap with gypsophila, then when it started to die back to underplant it with nasturtiums that hid its brown seed pods.

THE next time you buy a bunch of tulips or pick some from your garden, spare a thought for the seventeenth-century Dutchmen who won or lost fortunes over just a few bulbs. Bulbs were even offered on the London Stock Exchange in 1636, such was the intensity of tulipomania at its height.

24

LILIUM REGALE AND THE
EVERLASTING SWEETPEA (THE
PERENNIAL *LATHYRUS GRANDIFLORA*)
MINGLE WITH ROSES, PLUMBAGO
AND THE FIRST SUMMER CHERRIES IN
THIS COTTAGE WINDOW.

It all started in sixteenth-century Turkey, where the tulip was cultivated and greatly admired. There were tulip festivals and even official state growers, and when Busbecq, the Viennese ambassador to the court of Suleiman the Magnificent, saw the tulips in around 1554 it is believed he soon sent some bulbs back to Ferdinand I in Germany. The first tulip flowered there five years later, and an illustration and description of the flower appeared the following year. Suddenly, everyone wanted to grow what the English botanist Gerard later called these 'strange and forreine' flowers. The treasured bulbs arrived in England in 1578, and John Parkinson wrote of the tulip 'There is no lady or gentleman of any worth that is not caught with their delight'. By the seventeenth cen-

I LIKE THE IDEA OF BEING ABLE TO SEE STALKS THROUGH A GLASS VASE, AND THESE BOLD POLKA DOTS ON THE FABRIC MAKE NEW SHAPES WHENEVER THE VASE IS MOVED. THE SIMPLICITY OF THE NARCISSI IS BEAUTIFULLY CONTRASTED BY THE POLKA DOTS. USED IN SMALL AMOUNTS OR AS A MASS OF DIFFERENT VARIETIES, NARCISSI ARE A MORE THAN WELCOME SIGHT IN THE SPRING, WHETHER THEY ARE GROWING IN YOUR GARDEN OR FILLING A ROOM WITH THEIR DELICIOUS SCENT.

✧ ✧ ✧

Narcissi were grown by the ancient Egyptians and Greeks. They were also popular at the time of the Dutch tulipomania, although not to the same frenetic degree. Breeders introduced many fancy new forms, breeding them from their simple wild cousins which can be much more beautiful and precious.

❧

tury all manner of colours and varieties were available – at a price – but they were all striped. Plain coloured tulips were just used for breeding stock and weren't appreciated in their own right at all. Ironically enough, what the tulipomanes didn't realize was that the stripes they coveted so dearly are actually caused by a virus spread by aphids, and can eventually damage the vigour of the bulb.

Tulipomania really flourished between 1634 and 1637, during which time noblemen speculated on the bulbs with varying degrees of success. A single bulb of the red and white striped tulip 'Semper Augustus' was sold for 5,000 Dutch florins and a carriage and pair. Of course, the mania couldn't and didn't last, although there were revivals in Turkey and Holland during the eighteenth century, and a catalogue of 1854 listed three bulbs for sale at 100 guineas each. Instead, tulips became the preserve of florists – people who specialized in growing and exhibiting particular plants. In the seventeenth century they had mostly been wealthy, but by the nineteenth century they were usually green-fingered industrial workers. Tulips also appeared in cottage gardens, and you can still buy many old varieties, as well as a host of new ones.

'ROSES, roses, all the way.' So wrote Robert Browning, and it is a sentiment I agree with wholeheartedly. There must be a rose to suit every taste, from the species roses with their tiny flowers

SIMPLICITY

THIS WOODEN BASKET LOOKS
RATHER LIKE A LOW UNPAINTED
PICKET FENCE WITH ROSES GROWING
OVER IT, ALTHOUGH THE BOTTLE IN
THE BACKGROUND AND THE
CHEQUERED CLOTH GIVE A SENSE OF
SCALE. FILLING A BASKET LIKE THIS
WITH ROSE HEADS WILL LOOK
WONDERFUL BUT THE ROSES WON'T
LAST FOR LONG OUT OF WATER.
UNLESS YOU HAVE SO MANY ROSES
THAT YOU CAN HAPPILY ALLOW A
COUPLE OF DOZEN TO DIE OF THIRST
(WHICH SEEMS CRUEL IN THE
EXTREME), YOU WILL HAVE TO
DISGUISE THE CONTAINERS INSIDE
THE BASKET. THE BEST WAY TO DO
THIS IS TO USE SEVERAL SMALL
GLASS JARS OR VASES AND
CAMOUFLAGE THEM WITH ROSE
HEADS. THE ROSES CAN THEN BE
ARRANGED IN THE CONTAINERS,
PERHAPS WITH A FEW LEAVES
INTERSPERSED BETWEEN THE HEADS
TO HIDE ANY GLASS RIMS FROM
PRYING EYES.

28

RIGHT   YOU CAN HAPPILY COMBINE
FLORIST FLOWERS AND GARDEN
BLOOMS. HERE THE SOFTNESS OF THE
TREE MALLOW (*LAVATERA*
'BARNSLEY') AND GARDEN ROSES
BLEND PERFECTLY WITH
ALSTROEMERIA, ARUM LILIES
(*ZANTEDESCHIA*), STOCKS AND
LILIES. THIS VARIED SELECTION OF
FLOWERS CREATES A SIMPLE THEME
OF CREAM, PEACH AND PINK.

FACING PAGE   HERE IS A
PROVENÇAL-STYLE COLLECTION OF
GARDEN ROSES WHICH ECHOES THE
SIMPLICITY OF COUNTRY LIFE.
I CHOSE VASES OF VARYING HEIGHTS
AND DESIGNS TO INCREASE THE
INTEREST OF THE ARRANGEMENT,
AND PLACED THEM ALL ON AN OLD
TIN TRAY TO HOLD THEM TOGETHER.

and equally miniature leaves and the neat, well-behaved hybrid teas to the blousy centifolias that shed their many petals at the first touch of rain and the languid ramblers that hang their heads, unable to support the weight of their copious flowers. Along the way are damasks, gallicas, chinas, albas, musks, mosses, bourbons, noisettes, rugosas, floribundas, climbers and many other groups of roses, and they have all played their part in the development and cultivation of the roses we know today.

Exuberance

...FLOWERS AZURE, BLACK AND STREAKED WITH GOLD,
FAIRER THAN ANY WAKENED EYES BEHOLD.
from *The Question*, Percy Bysshe Shelley

PREVIOUS PAGE SO MANY OF THE
POT POURRIS ON SALE EITHER LOOK
DUSTY OR GARISH, WITH A HARSH
ARTIFICIAL SMELL, AND THEY SIMPLY
AREN'T WORTH BUYING. INSTEAD,
YOU CAN MAKE YOUR OWN FROM A
COLLECTION OF THE FLOWERS AND
FOLIAGE IN YOUR GARDEN. THIS
SELECTION OF DRIED ROSE BUDS,
DELPHINIUM HEADS, GERANIUM
LEAVES, CINNAMON STICKS, CLOVES,
SLIVERS OF ORANGE PEEL AND TINY
CRAB APPLES SHOWS PERFECTLY
THAT POT POURRI CAN BE
ANYTHING BUT DULL.

✤ ✤ ✤

Blanket flowers, with their
hairy stems, cling very
obediently to their neighbours
in a vase and are a
joy to arrange.

❧

EXUBERANCE brings to mind the mystical time of harvest when churches and homes are profusely adorned with offerings of the season's bounty. The ancient Greeks and Romans had gods who ruled over this time of year and were worshipped in the hope that they would show their pleasure with a plentiful harvest. Times have changed and at the close of the twentieth century we are more inclined to put our trust in chemical fertilizers and disease-resistant plants than the good graces of the gods, with damaging and unsightly results.

An exuberant sense of style must surely have reached its zenith during the sixteenth and seventeenth centuries, and is reflected in the still lives that were painted so superbly by Dutch, Flemish, Italians and Spanish artists. Serenity and wonder are combined with lavish expressions of the season in these magnificent paintings. Cherries tumble over figs, and butterflies and bees decorate myriad flowers of every colour and variety with little regard for their proper seasons. Looking at paintings like these will help you to develop a more flamboyant eye for flowers and encourage you to experiment with style.

For sheer inspiration I can recommend a visit to your local flower market early one morning, simply so you can enjoy and be overwhelmed by the colours of the flowers. In fact, I think this is an important ritual – and, indeed, a necessity – for any flower lover. You will see colours laid over colours, with so many differ-

ent ones massed together they will dazzle you. When you are satiated and have to leave there will always be another visit to look forward to, with more varieties and fresh supplies to tantalize you. Seeing so much variety will encourage you to buy in abundance, and that is true of any market where spices, fruit, vegetables or flowers are in profusion.

One of the joys of a large flower market is seeing masses of flowers which have been flown in from abroad and are often ahead of their season at home. It is exhilarating and fills one with a sense of hope to see the delicate lemon-yellow heads of narcissi on a dark winter's morning for they herald the promise of spring. However, if you want to create a sense of floral exuberance without breaking the bank you will do better to buy flowers in their correct season, especially if you long to fill every room in your home.

THIS VASE OF BLANKET FLOWERS (GAILLARDIA) IS AN IDEAL EXAMPLE OF THE FUN IT CAN BE TO MATCH THE FLOWER TO THE CONTAINER. THE DABS OF COLOUR ON THE PETALS BLEND WITH THE PLAYFUL SPLASHES OF COLOUR ON THE VASE. YOU MIGHT EVEN LIKE TO TRY PAINTING YOUR OWN VASE TO MATCH YOUR FAVOURITE FLOWERS, AS A WIDE VARIETY OF CERAMIC COLOURS IS NOW AVAILABLE.

Gypsophila, sprays of asters and soapwort (*Saponaria*) will help to fill out the vases, especially when mixed with the voluminous blooms of paeonies, hydrangeas, sunflowers and the prima donna ballgown of the flower world, the giant oriental poppy (*Papaver orientalis*).

You can use combinations of flowers to create the effect of a Persian carpet, choosing colours and varieties of a jewel-like quality, such as Sweet Williams with ranunculas, small garden scabious, Shirley poppies and some splashy tiger lilies. With such a sweep of luxury, life becomes a celebration once more and a gesture of thanks to Mother Nature.

TULIPS were so highly revered in eighteenth-century Turkey that special tulip gardens were laid out by Ahmed III in his Topkapi Palace. Lavish night parties were held each year when the tulips came into bloom, with the flowers illuminated not only by lamps but also by tortoises, with tiny lanterns attached to their shells, which ambled about the paths. It is claimed that sometimes the tulips were torn to shreds by women who were jealous of the flowers' beauty.

SUMMER is definitely the season of exuberance, when flowers bloom their hearts out. Colours are bright and vivid to stand up to the strong sunlight, and bees become drunk on the nectar they have gath-

ered from so many plants. You just have to let the sunshine in with zinnias, *Cosmos*, marigolds and nasturtiums, for only once a year does Nature let her guard down and shower us with unrestrained excess. You can happily pick armfuls of flowers from your garden and cram vases and jars with them, safe in the knowledge that many more will soon take their place. There is no need to restrict yourself to flowers, of course, and you might like to echo the Flemish painters of the seventeenth and eighteenth centuries by including little sprays of strawberries amongst your flowers, cherry tomatoes, branches of lemons or blackberries. You could also use flowering sprigs of the more unusual bullace (*Prunus domestica*), which was once grown as a cultivated plum and has now been superseded by better varieties.

You can also make colourful pot pourris with summer flowers, and it is lovely to place bowls of homemade pot pourri about the house. Roses and lavender keep their perfume even when they have been dried, long after all other flowers have given up their last vestige of scent. To make a pot pourri, dried flowers and leaves are mixed with powdered orris root (the underground root of a particular species of iris), which acts as a fixative for the aromatic essential oils that are also added.

I use flowers and herbs from my own garden to make pot pourri like the one shown on pages 32-3, picking apple mint, roses, rosemary, lavender and jas-

ROSES SCATTERED OVER A FAVOURITE PIECE OF ANTIQUE SATIN RIBBON (AN EXCITING FIND AT AN ANTIQUES SHOW) PRODUCE AN UTTERLY FEMININE BLEND OF LATE-SUMMER SUNLIGHT AND SILKY TEXTURES. CUT ROSES – ESPECIALLY LARGE, OVERBLOWN ONES – MAKE A STRIKING ADDITION TO A SUMMER HAT OR JACKET.

❧ ❧ ❧

If you are unlucky enough to get a rose thorn stuck in your finger, applying a thick paste of water and bicarbonate of soda to the affected area and leaving it there for a while will help draw out the offending barb. A long hot soak in the bath can also serve the same purpose.

mine for the base and adding other flowers as they come into season. Placing complete flower heads on top of the pot pourri is an excellent way to improve its texture and appearance. When my delphiniums have passed their prime but long before they are dying, I pick off the best of the remaining flower heads because their heavenly blues are the perfect complement to the faded pinks and mauves of my pot pourri. Arrange them in large wide bowls and you will still be enjoying the scents of summer long after that season has passed.

ROSES are soft and sensual to the touch, belying the potential viciousness that often lies in wait among their stems. I love the story in Roman mythology that tells how the rose originally got its thorns. Careless Cupid, the son of Venus, goddess of love, was one day stung by a bee and he responded immediately by firing an arrow through a nearby rose, thereby endowing it for ever more with thorns. Mere mortals may be reminded of Cupid's timely dart if, like me, they plant roses too near a path. I made this mistake once by placing some roses near my French windows and, although it was delightful to sit on the back steps and be seduced by their perfume, their close proximity caused many a stab to my unwary and unprotected legs.

A leisurely browse through a good book on roses will reveal many roses that have few thorns or even

A MASS OF DIFFERENT ORCHIDS
PRODUCES A DAZZLING EXPRESSION
OF PURE JOY AND SHOWS MY LOVE
OF COLOUR. THE ORCHIDS INCLUDE
CYMBIDIUM 'LITTLE BIG HORN',
PHALAENOPSIS AND VARIOUS
ORIENTAL ORCHIDS.

none at all, such as the lovely old bourbon 'Zéphirine Drouhin' and are therefore ideal for planting by paths or around doorways. Other roses bristle with thorns, making the perfect defence against unwelcome intruders: *Rosa sericea* and 'Constance Spry' are two very different roses with equally cruel thorns.

ORCHIDS are among the most exotic flowers in the world, astonishing in their colours, shapes and sizes. Some of them have flowers that look like tatters of red, orange or green ribbon, some like white and yellow irises or narcissi, while others are extraordinary, flamboyant painted sculptures that seem to defy gravity and even reason. The more one gazes at them the more one wonders why on earth they are shaped in the way they are and what insects they are trying to attract.

Their exotic beauty gives the impression that orchids are difficult to grow but that isn't always the case and some happily thrive indoors as house plants. Others need the humidity of the greenhouse and more specialized care, but even if you can't or don't want to grow them yourself that is no reason for not using them in flower arrangements. They will last a very long time provided you keep them supplied with plenty of fresh water.

Victorians were especially fond of wearing orchids in their buttonholes or as corsages, because they recognized them as the true aristocrats of the flower world.

Now the lusty spring is seen;
  Golden yellow, gaudy blue,
  Daintily invite the view:
Everywhere on every green
Roses blushing as they blow
  And enticing men to pull,
Lilies whiter than the snow,
  Woodbines of sweet honey full:
  All love's emblems, and all cry,
  'Ladies, if not plucked, we die'.

from *Love's Emblems*, John Fletcher

THIS COMBINATION OF TWO VERY
DIFFERENT FLOWERS – STATICE
(*LIMONIUM SUWOROWII*) AND ARUM
LILIES (*ZANTEDESCHIA*) – PROVES
THE LATE CONSTANCE SPRY'S
THEORY THAT THERE ARE NO TWO
FLOWERS THAT CANNOT BE PUT
TOGETHER.

PRUNUS is a genus of over 430 species of mainly trees and shrubs, but the ornamental species includes almond, peach, plum and cherry trees. These trees are wonderful harbingers of spring, for as their flower buds grow and swell one knows that spring is just around the corner, and that it has definitely arrived when the trees are decked in their heavenly blossom, which they scatter in a light breeze.

Some of the trees have the added advantage of producing scented blossom, and then it is almost impossible to resist the temptation of picking a few branches for the house. If the tree is a fruit-bearing one and not just ornamental, cutting branches of blossom will of course reduce your crop of fruit but that seems a very small price to pay for the sheer joy of seeing and smelling a vase filled with a fragrant cloud of petals.

The flowers of the different *Prunus* trees (both ornamental and fruit-bearing) vary considerably, from small delicate single flowers to generous clusters of pink pompons or what look like miniature roses. No wonder these trees appear in so many Japanese paintings. John Evelyn wrote that wild cherries 'thrive into stately trees, beautified with blossoms of a surprising whiteness, greatly relieving the sedulous bees'.

PEOPLE often have a favourite colour which comes through not only in the clothes they choose to wear and how they chose to decorate their interiors but also extends to their choice of flowers.

꙼ ꙼ ꙼

. . . Nor can I find, amid my
lonely walk
By rivulet, or spring, or wet
roadside
That blue and bright-eyed
flowerlet of the brook,
Hope's gentle gem, the sweet
Forget-me-not!

The Keepsake, Samuel Taylor
Coleridge

Mine most definitely is blue. I cannot seem to avoid it, even if I wanted to, and find that I am drawn to it again and again.

My love affair with blue flowers began with forget-me-nots (*Myosotis*), which I had growing like a blue sea in my first garden in spring. Interestingly enough, the forget-me-not has the same meaning in French (where it is called *ne m'oubliez pas*) and German (*vergiss mein nicht*), and tradition says that when you wear the forget-me-not you are not forgotten by your love. There is a charming German story of a knight and his lady who were walking by a river. As the knight bent down to pick some forget-me-nots he fell into the river, but managed to throw the flowers to his lady, crying '*vergiss mein nicht*' before he was swept away by the current and drowned. One of the joys of growing these lovely flowers is their happy habit of seeding

YOU CAN ALMOST HEAR THE BLACKBIRDS SING IN THIS PICTURE OF JAPANESE AND ORNAMENTAL CHERRY BLOSSOM. IT IS A DELIGHTFUL SIGHT IN SPRING WHEN, PERHAPS AFTER A SLIGHT SHOWER, THE PETALS COVER LAWNS AND STREETS WITH PINK CONFETTI.

themselves freely around the garden, so one small plant will quickly multiply itself to form a marvellous swathe of tiny, delicate, blue flowers.

SOME flowers are so intricate that they are best viewed close up rather than from afar, and I love floating exotic flower heads in water so I can gaze down on them and really study their markings. Arranging a few flowers in low dishes is a good idea for a dinner party because you are able to decorate the table *and* provide an uninterrupted view.

Mixed orchids lying in a shallow dish of water can look almost like a piece of embroidery or wrapping paper and will be a source of endless fascination both for you and your guests. You can use as many or as few flowers as you like for this type of arrangement, but it is particularly successful if you leave plenty of space around each flower so it can be viewed without distractions. Lilies, camellias, gardenias and simpler flowers such as primroses or pansies all benefit from this treatment. All you must do is ensure the shallow bowls of water don't dry up, which will quickly happen in a warm room if you aren't paying attention to them.

SOME flowers are so exuberant you can almost paint with them, as I have done in the photograph on the facing page. I love gerberas for their vivid, marvellously clear colours and stunning perfec-

HERE I TOOK THE FADING PETALS
FROM SOME GERBERAS AND PLACED
THEM ON A PURPLE MAT,
ARRANGING THEM LIKE FRESH
BRUSHSTROKES OF PURE PAINT
SQUEEZED STRAIGHT FROM THE
TUBE. I ADDED A FERN LEAF TO
GIVE A CONTRAST OF
COLOUR AND SHAPE.

tion of shape, but I think for sheer exuberance in a flower, nothing in the plant kingdom can match the dahlia.

She is a mysterious lady, for hidden behind her brave winning smile lies a delicate nature. Her tubers must not feel a trace of frost or fungus otherwise they will wither and die, and she craves sunshine and a well-drained situation. However, if you abide by those considerations and give your dahlias the conditions they need, they will reward you by being some of the easiest summer flowers to grow. If you live in a place with cold, wet winters you will have to lift and store the tubers in boxes of sand in a frost-free place when the dahlias have finished flowering, then replant them the following year when all danger of frost is past, but that is little trouble for a garden full of sunny spectacular dahlias the following summer. If frost is not a problem, your dahlias can stay in the ground the whole year long, although you may have to dig up and divide the tubers occasionally to give new life and vigour to the plants – and increase your stock.

Spot-planting dahlias in a mixed herbaceous border is not always advisable as they seem to resent competition and dislike having to fight for their existence with other flowers. These sunny creatures prefer their own space, so a more satisfactory solution is to give them a corner or whole bed entirely devoted to their needs. Don't forget to stake them, otherwise a strong

Playtime with petals can take you back to being a child again, to be mesmerized by texture and colour and to recapture a sense of awe.

EXUBERANCE

THE GOLDEN-RAYED LILY OF JAPAN
(*LILIUM AURATUM*), SHOWN HERE IN
A SMALL BOWL, HAS A RICH, SPICY
FRAGRANCE THAT IS THE PERFECT
COMPLEMENT TO ITS BREATHTAKING
BEAUTY. THE FACT THAT IT IS EASY
TO GROW AND ADDS GREAT
DISTINCTION AND GRACE TO ANY
FLOWER ARRANGEMENT IS A BONUS.
FOR ME, IT CLAIMS FULL MARKS FOR
SUPERB SHAPE, COLOUR, PERFUME
AND DIGNITY. IN THIS
ARRANGEMENT, I HAVE PUT IT
WITH BOUGAINVILLEA AND
CORNFLOWER PETALS.

AT FIRST GLANCE IT IS HARD TO
SEE WHERE THE DAHLIA STOPS AND
THE VASE STARTS, WHICH IS
PRECISELY WHY I CHOSE IT. USING A
CONTAINER THAT MIMICS THE FORM
OF THE FLOWER IT HOLDS CAN BE
VERY VISUALLY EXCITING.

wind will blow them about and snap their stalks.

Dahlias vary considerably in shape, and are divided into different groups according to their flower heads: anemone, collerette, decorative, ball, cactus, pompon and water-lily are just some of them. Water-lily dahlias are among my favourites because of their robust natures and open star faces. When picked for an arrangement they look best cut short so they can float in a bowl of water like the aquatic sisters after which they are named.

Bi-coloured decoratives provide a staggering selection of colours from which to choose and I love them for their broad petals of broken colour, where one colour is tipped with another and accents of red punctuate dabs of white, cream is splashed on to orange and yellow is daubed over pink to a truly riotous effect. These magnificent plants have been tenderly

I LOVE THE SPIKINESS OF DAHLIAS,
AND ARRANGING THEM LIKE THIS
MAKES THEM LOOK LIKE MULTI-
COLOURED SEA URCHINS RATHER
THAN FLOWERS. DISPLAYING SINGLE
BLOOMS REALLY SHOWS THEM
OFF AND LETS THEM TAKE
CENTRE STAGE.

grown and shown by enthusiasts for many years, but I think with careful planting the exciting colours and textures of these magical dahlias can be elevated from their old associations of muddy boots and allotments to the pinnacle where they really belong. They are true stars of the floral stage.

The Empress Josephine, renowned for her magnificent gardens at Malmaison and her love of roses, was also a passionate lover of dahlias. She had bought some very rare tubers from Spain and basked in the envy and compliments that showered her every summer when her treasured dahlias came into flower. Josephine didn't want anyone else to steal her thunder so she refused all requests for spare tubers. However, she hadn't bargained for the clever lady of her court who persuaded one of the gardeners to dig up

Dahlias were first found growing in Aztec gardens in Central America, yet may well have originally been taken to Europe and grown in gardens there as a vegetable! Dahlias reached Madrid in the eighteenth century and were distributed to other European countries during the 1780s.

some choice specimens for her. The following summer the stolen dahlias were revealed in all their flowering glory and a furious Josephine fired the gardener, banished the woman from her court and had all the dahlias dug up and destroyed. She never grew them again, and really seems to have cut off her nose to spite her face. It comes as no surprise to me that flowers can arouse such strong passions.

THIS LOOSE ARRANGEMENT OF BRILLIANTLY COLOURED GERBERAS ILLUSTRATES PERFECTLY HOW APPARENTLY INCOMPATIBLE COLOURS CAN BE COMBINED TO SPECTACULAR EFFECT. THE LARGE, UNIFORMLY VIBRANT GERBERA BLOOMS SEEM TO CRY OUT FOR SUCH EXTRAVAGANT TREATMENT AND HERE THE RED AND ORANGE, YELLOW AND PINK FLOWERS ARE OFFSET BY AN EQUALLY EXUBERANT PAINTED BACKDROP.

Gerberas can flower from summer to winter, depending on their growing conditions, but full sun and a light sandy soil are essential. There is a huge range of colours to choose from, with not only reds, oranges and yellows available but also tender apricots, pale pinks and soft creams.

Sophistication

MY GARDEN ALL IS OVERBLOWN WITH ROSES,
MY SPIRIT ALL IS OVERBLOWN WITH RHYME.

from *Sonnet*, Vita Sackville-West

PREVIOUS PAGES CASABLANCA LILIES STAND IN DAPPLED LIGHT, CREATING A SENSE OF QUIET CALM SOPHISTICATION. THE LARGE STAMENS OF LILIES LOOK VERY DRAMATIC BUT CAN STAIN SO MANY PEOPLE REMOVE THEM BUT I THINK THEY ARE PART OF THE STRIKING BEAUTY OF LILIES AND I PREFER THEIR GREAT BLOBS OF FLUFFY POLLEN TO BE SEEN.

RIGHT A VASE FILLED ONLY WITH THE *PHALAENOPSIS AMABILIS* ORCHID SHOWS THESE BEAUTIFUL FLOWERS OFF TO PERFECTION.

FACING PAGE FLECKED DAHLIAS ARE VAGUELY REMINISCENT OF APPLE BLOSSOM AND THEIR SPIKY PETALS MAKE A PLEASING CONTRAST WITH THE SENSUAL CURVES OF *LILIUM SPECIOSUM*. THE DARK PINK OF THE FLOWERS AND THE COBALT BLUE OF THE VASE LINKS UP WITH THE BACKGROUND TO TURN THE ARRANGEMENT INTO A COMPLETE PICTURE.

LOOK up the word 'sophistication' in the dictionary and you will get a confusing mixture of definitions. To me, though, true sophistication can be seen in the natural lines that are so perfectly expressed in Nature, and whose beauty would defeat the most ingenious draughtsman or craftsman. Nothing can compare with the stately spires of delphineums, the grand eloquence of the rose, the sensuality of bearded irises with their appearance of silky underwear, or Madonna lilies that hold themselves so proudly.

Careful combinations of flowers create a wide variety of moods and images and give tremendous satisfaction. Mediterranean flowers always seem to go well together, with mimosa, geraniums, jasmine, bougainvillea and plumbago all suggestive of wonderfully sunny climes. Carefree flower arrangements can be created

A SINGLE SKELETAL ASPEN LEAF STANDS IN DELICATE SIMPLICITY. A HUNT AROUND THE GARDEN IN AUTUMN AND WINTER CAN BE VERY REWARDING AND MAY PRODUCE SOME WONDERFUL SURPRISES. YOU CAN FIND LEAVES THAT HAVE BEEN REDUCED TO SKELETONS, REVEALING A SIMPLICITY AND BEAUTY THAT REPAYS CAREFUL SCRUTINY.

with a subtle sophisticated blend of more fragile flowers, with character, colour and shape as the determining factors. Astrantia, larkspur, Queen Anne's Lace, alchemilla, feverfew and *Solanum* are all eminently suitable flowers.

For a more distinctive mood you need the flourish of a single species, provided you have enough flowers. If only for the sheer indulgent delight of it, I thoroughly recommend buying a complete box of flowers. Be generous if you can, for there is nothing quite so heady and intoxicating as an armful of flowers, although being in love may come a close second!

Of course showers of flowers aren't essential in order to create something special. Elegant and striking flower arrangements can be made quite simply by a considered approach and appreciation of the flower. The contemplation of a single bloom gives that flower increased significance, and one white flower inspires a sense of purity and perfection. You can use a single Madonna lily (*Lilium candidum*), magnolia flower, white 'Iceberg' rose, sprig of cherry blossom or one Californian poppy (*Romneya coulteri*) for the purest expression of grace and beauty.

Small arrangements of flowers can often be intimate and comforting, whether it is a wine glass full of blue gentians in spring or a bowl of floating hellebores at Christmas. Even if you buy your flowers from a florist you may be able to pick foliage from the garden, and often the simplest leaves will give a comple-

SOPHISTICATION

A NOSTALGIC BLEND OF LEAVES AND
A CUSTARD MARROW CREATE A
SYMPHONY OF MONOCHROMATIC
COLOUR WHICH FOOLS US INTO
THINKING IT MUST HAVE RECEIVED
A COLOUR WASH OF SIENNA. LEAVES
CAN BE SOAKED IN A MIXTURE OF
WATER AND BORAX TO STRIP THEM,
ALTHOUGH IN WINTER YOU MIGHT
FIND SKELETAL PODS OF CHINESE
LANTERNS (*PHYSALIS*) OR HOLLY
LEAVES WHICH HAVE BEEN
ATTACKED BY FROST OR SLUGS AND
STRIPPED TO THEIR SILVERY BONES.
THEY MAKE DELIGHTFUL
DECORATIONS FOR CHRISTMAS.

69

PREVIOUS PAGES OPINION IS DIVIDED ON HOW TO DRY THE MARVELLOUS *HYDRANGEA MACROPHYLLA*, PRESUMABLY BECAUSE THERE IS NO SINGLE METHOD THAT GUARANTEES SUCCESSFUL RESULTS. WHEN I WANT TO DRY THESE HUGE HYDRANGEA HEADS I HEDGE MY BETS JUST TO BE ON THE SAFE SIDE. I DRY HALF THE BUNCH IN WATER, THEREBY ALLOWING THE FLOWERS TO PASS FROM LIFE TO DEATH AT A SLOW PACE, AND DRY THE OTHER HALF IN A VASE WITHOUT ANY WATER. MANY FLOWERS CAN BE HUNG UP TO DRY BUT THIS PROCESS SEEMS TO MAKE HYDRANGEA FLOWERS CURL UP.

mentary subtlety to your flowers. Pittosporum, trailing ivy, rue, euonymus, ferns and the bright green of spurge (*Euphorbia robbiae*) are all excellent choices.

HERBS play a special part in any garden, large or small, and are very easy to grow and rewarding to look at. They are also more than useful for pot pourri, cooking and scenting the linen cupboard or bath water. I find them essential in the garden, not only for their culinary uses but also their decorative and olfactory ones. I used to grow thyme along the edge of a garden path and always seemed to need a few sprigs when it was raining, but I didn't mind braving the wet because the sweet smell of the herb more than made up for any inconvenience.

A sprinkling of lavender or lemon-scented verbena leaves can be used to perfume your bath water, or you could choose the leaves of one of the many aromatic geraniums (*Pelargoniums*), the scents of which include pineapple, lemon, peppermint and rose. Alternatively you could use sprigs of rosemary, which is astringent and antiseptic, French rose petals or even my favourite, oleander petals. After a hard day's gardening what could be more indulgent than a candlelit bath and a glass of wine to soothe away those aches and pains.

Purple sage, borage and eau de Cologne mint are delightful additions to bouquets of flowers. For my birthday every year a friend used to give me a tiny posy of the first moss rose surrounded by eau de Cologne mint. It was a wonderful combination of perfumes and I always think of her now when I smell mint.

Herbs are also extremely useful companion plants in the garden so shouldn't be confined to a single herb bed. Clever gardeners will plant particular herbs next to certain flowers in the knowledge that the herb will deter that flowers' insect predators. It is no co-incidence that rose bushes are often underplanted with alliums: the greenfly that find roses so delicious can't abide the oniony smell of the alliums and will therefore fly off to infest someone else's roses instead of your own. A few nasturtiums (especially if planted

LEFT   A SINGLE ANGELICA HEAD, SHAPED LIKE A HUGE BURST OF GREEN FIREWORKS, ACCOMPANIES A BOWL OF MIXED HERBS WHICH INCLUDE SAGE, ROSEMARY AND A SCENTED GERANIUM.

A little angelica leaf can be used in baking and is a wonderful addition to apple pie. The young stems can be crystallized to make the sugary twigs of candied angelica.

73

in tubs) will attract all the local blackfly in droves, thereby keeping them away from your more precious plants. What is more, some plants and herbs are such good friends that they encourage each other to grow in the most lavish profusion.

MOST lilies are easy to grow and make a wonderful addition to any garden. They provide an excellent focal point, especially if clustered around an ancient pot, piece of sculpture, corner of the garden or end of a pathway. Their elegance and heady perfume confirm their rightful status in the flower world – and an undisputed place in the most simple or sophisticated of settings.

It is useful to remember, if you are fond of lilies as I am, to buy good virus-free stock and to choose varieties that will bloom during different months of the year, thus assuring an extended flowering season and in effect staggering your planting. You may choose the graceful Madonna lily (*Lilium candidum*), grown for three and a half thousand years, for early flowering, the simple regal lily (*L. regale*) to follow on and the splendid golden-rayed lily of Japan (*L. auratum*) to finish the season in style.

Lilies make delightful pot plants for the home or conservatory but you must never let their compost dry out. I find it kindest to the bulbs to line the containers with sheets of plastic (you can cut up sturdy plastic bags) before filling them with compost, to stop

the sun drying out the pots too quickly — especially small pots.

Lilies are greedy feeders. An ideal spring tonic is a mixture of peat, well-rotted manure and a little bone meal, either carefully forked into the soil around lilies grown in the garden, or to replace some of the existing compost in containers. Take care to stake late-flowering lilies, or those growing in especially windy sites, otherwise gusts of wind or autumn gales could

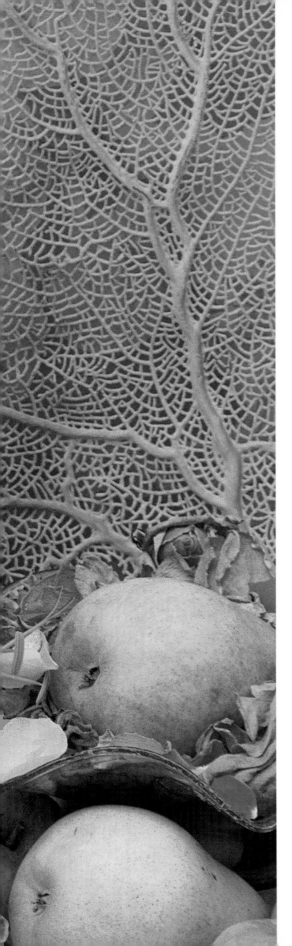

A Sensitive Plant in a garden grew,
And the young winds fed it with
silver dew,
And it opened its fan – like leaves to
the light,
And closed them beneath the kisses of
night.

And the Spring arose on the garden
fair,
Like the Spirit of Love felt
everywhere;
And each flower and herb on Earth's
dark breast
Rose fresh from the dreams of its
wintry nest.

from *The Sensitive Plant*, Percy Bysshe Shelley

I LOVE THE RICHNESS OF THIS
PHOTOGRAPH, WITH THE YELLOW
RIBBONS OF COLOUR RUNNING
DOWN THE PETALS OF THE APTLY
NAMED GLORY LILY (*GLORIOSA
SUPERBA* 'ROTHSCHILDIANA'). THE
POMEGRANATES ECHO THE ROUNDED
SHAPE OF THE FLOWERS AND THE
WARMTH OF THEIR COLOURING.

ꗉ ꗉ ꗉ

The name *Papaver* is taken from the Latin word Papa, meaning 'father'. An ancient potion, used to lull babies to sleep, was made from the seeds or milky sap of this plant.

ꔛ

prove too much for their heavy flower heads.

Most lilies aren't fussy about the type of soil in which they are grown, provided it is well-drained, but a few do have more specific needs. The Madonna lily and *L. henrii*, for example, both love very alkaline soil, while *L. speciosum* and the Turkscap lily (*L. superbum*) require a neutral to acid soil. I don't want to make it sound as though these wonderful bulbs are difficult to grow, because if you give them their favourite conditions they will thank you by coming up year after year, spreading themselves underground and filling your garden or greenhouse with magnificent colour and scent. I well remember my delight and shock when a collection of *L. speciosum* finally blushed away in a corner of my small garden.

Arranging lilies in a vase can be quite a challenge because their straight stems will willingly go into rigid postures, but who wants a rigid flower arrangement? The trick is to make them appear soft and sensual, and if you use several stems they will support each other and allow you to play around with their different curves and inclinations. Delphiniums, orchids, irises, agapanthus and nerines are other straight-stemmed flowers that need to be gently coaxed into place, so use the same technique for them them too.

Lilies are so beautiful that it makes sense to prolong their lives as cut flowers for as long as possible, and you can do this by changing their vase water

A SINGLE ORCHID (*PAPHIOPEDILUM* 'ALMAND') IS THE HEIGHT OF SOPHISTICATION. CUTTING THE STEM OF THE ORCHID SO THE FLOWER SITS JUST ABOVE THE NECK OF THE VASE INCREASES THE DRAMA OF THE ARRANGEMENT AND ALSO THE SENSE OF MYSTERY.

every day and frequently cutting about 5 cm (2 in) off the ends of their stems, which will not only give them renewed vitality but also encourage the smaller flower buds to open. If you want some cut lilies for a special occasion do make sure that you buy them a couple of days in advance to give them plenty of time to come into flower.

HIGHLY pleasing, and therefore successful, ideas can be sophisticated if they involve understatement. That is true of the elegant suit or a piece of sculpture, and so it is with some flowers, such as a single orchid.

Like lilies, orchids are so beautiful and exotic that one might think they are very difficult to grow, but in fact many can be cultivated in a frost-free greenhouse, or even grown in the border during the summer months. What they cannot abide are severe frosts (although some of them can't stand any type of frost at all), becoming frozen in their pots or being water-logged, so you must take great care not to expose them to any of these hazards. Even so, many orchids are remarkably tolerant and can withstand a little neglect.

Paphiopedilum orchids, such as the one shown on the facing page, need a warm, shady and humid situation to do well. A bathroom shelf and a little patience will ensure a long life, but do use a special orchid compost for the best results. I think one of the

Orchids like this one can be grown at home in the right conditions, but they are also available from florists. This spectacular flower will last for up to three months in water.

THE BRIGHT COLOURS OF THIS VASE
ECHO THE WAVES OF PINK AND
YELLOW PRESENT IN THE TULIPS.
POSITIVE MODERN COLOURS, SUCH
AS THESE, SHOULD NOT BE AVOIDED
AS THEIR RICHNESS CAN BRING JOY
TO ANY ROOM.

joys of growing plants is watching them thrive under one's care, and if your orchids enjoy living with you they will put out lots of new growth. *Paphiopedilum* orchids produce this new growth from the base, and so can be divided in spring into three plants when there are six new growths. This is a wonderfully exciting and satisfying way of increasing your stock, and if you wish you can pass your good fortune on to friends by giving away the new orchids as presents.

Although the plant has nothing to do with sex its name is derived from the Greek *orkhis*, meaning testicle (which refers to the shape of its tubers). In herbals of the fifteenth century, the orchid bulb was frequently recommended as an aphrodisiac, and special recipes were given for combining the bulb with the brains of sparrows or pigeons, stag truffles, spices and the odd fungus. The medieval belief in the Doctrine of Signatures linked man and Nature: if a plant resembled a part of the human body it was presumed to have some curative or healing effect on it.

I LOVE to use just flowers in my arrangements, whether there are masses of them cascading out of vases or a single bloom is sitting in solitary splendour. The explosion of tulips shown on the facing page is just the sort of arrangement I love because it bursts with vitality and intensity and is guaranteed to bring a smile to the face. The vase is full of the tulips and I think adding any other flowers or foliage would spoil

THIS PHOTOGRAPH SURELY PROVES
THAT YOU DON'T ALWAYS HAVE TO
PUT FLOWERS IN A VASE. I THINK
THIS IS A HIGHLY SOPHISTICATED
ARRANGEMENT BECAUSE IT ALLOWS
THE LEAVES TO SPEAK FOR
THEMSELVES AND SHOWS OFF THEIR
BEAUTIFUL SHAPE AND
FASCINATING TEXTURE.

Leaves absorb nourishment and
moisture through their
undersides, so it is beneficial
to spray your favourite plants
with liquid food every now and
then. I find the plant foods
based on seaweed are the best
and I must confess even to
spraying my roses on early
summer evenings in the hope of
ensuring their perfect health.

the atmosphere of the arrangement completely.

Many traditional flower arrangers, on the other hand, like to use foliage in all their work – something that is purely a matter of taste but definitely not mine. Instead of placing flowers and foliage in the same vase I prefer to use them separately, because many leaves are just as beautiful as flowers. Some of them have magnificent markings, such as those of the elegant hosta, which can be dark green edged with white or gold, streaked with lime green or decorated with central splodges of white.

The lovely furry leaves of lady's mantle (*Alchemilla mollis*) look breathtaking after a shower of rain, when the rain drops are caught on them like so many beads of mercury. In his *Herbal* of 1568, the writer William Turner wrote 'In the night it closeth it selfe together lyke a purse, and in the morning it is found ful of dewe'. You could reproduce this charming sight indoors by placing a few leaves in a vase and dropping a little water on them.

The white-spotted leaves of lungwort (*Pulmonaria*) are also beautiful in their own right. They really start to grow once the tiny flowers of this lovely plant have finished blooming in the spring, when they multiply fast to produce a thick carpet of leaves. Incidentally, the plant gets its common name because medieval doctors, following the Doctrine of Signatures, believed the white spots on the leaves represented spots on the lungs and that the plant was therefore

IT IS GREAT FUN TO USE ONE LARGE
DARING BLOOM AND HAVE A
GALAXY OF STARRY FLOWERS
SURROUNDING IT, AS I HAVE DONE
HERE WITH A SINGLE *HIPPEASTRUM*
FLOWER AND LOTS OF PINK AND
WHITE PARROT TULIPS.

excellent for treating diseases of the lungs. A far less prosaic fancy was that the leaves had become spotted when the Virgin Mary's tears or milk fell on them.

WHEN grouped together, *Hippeastrum* make an impressive and sophisticated addition to any room in spring. They look most effective when grown in very large bowls, like the old terracotta bowls that were once used for making bread. Do give them enough space in which to grow because if the bulbs are set too close together one bulb will dominate the other and so rob it of moisture and food.

The more you feed these greedy bulbs the more flower heads you will have, so include a little liquid feed whenever you water them (which should be as often as needed – *Hippeastrum* are thirsty creatures as well as hungry ones). If you are growing them indoors, where they certainly brighten up a room, you should cover the top of the compost with some damp sphagnum moss to act as a mulch and prevent too much moisture escaping into the air, and also to give a good finish to the bowl.

Many people seem to think that bulbs only grow in the spring, when there are certainly plenty in flower, and don't realize there are bulbs for most months of the year, such as lilies, anemones and freesias for the summer and special snowdrops and crocuses for the autumn. Many of the flowers are supremely sophisticated, although the same may not always be said for their leaves, which are often strap-like and can flop about in a very untidy way when flowering is over.

I have already written about some of my favourite bulbs in this book but there are many more that deserve a mention and fit well into this chapter. Crown imperials (*Fritillaria imperialis*) are magnificent plants that grow up to 1.5 metres (5 feet) tall and give an elegant feel to any spring border. They are very old plants, having arrived in Europe from Turkey and Persia in 1576. Crown imperials bear tufts of glossy leaves at the top of their long stems with vivid orange or yellow bells hanging beneath them. Their

Unusual combinations of flowers which show their contrasting textures include soapwort (*Saponaria*) with a single protea, an Oriental poppy surrounded by sweet peas or one gigantic sunflower with clouds of yellow mimosa around it.

SOPHISTICATION

IN THE BEAUTIFUL AND FANCIFUL
STORY OF ROMAN MYTHOLOGY,
FLORA, THE GODDESS OF FLOWERS,
YOUTH AND SPRING, IS SAID TO
HAVE CHANGED THE CHILD POET
CYANOS INTO A CORNFLOWER AFTER
HIS DEATH, SO HUMANITY WOULD
FOREVER BE REMINDED OF THE
LITTLE POET WHO SO SWEETLY SANG
THE PRAISES OF NATURE.

smaller cousin, the black sarana (*F. camschatcensis*) has fewer leaves but more flowers of a rich exotic blackish-purple colour.

The giant lily (*Cardiocrinum giganteum*) grows to a staggering 3 metres (10 feet) over several years and eventually bears huge creamy trumpet-shaped flowers in the summer. It is hardly surprising that, exhausted by such a lavish display, the main bulb dies after flowering but you can salvage its offset bulbs and grow them on until they finally come into flower themselves. On a less grand scale are the lovely *Crinum* X *powellii* bulbs which produce fragrant trumpet-shaped flower in late summer and early autumn.

Early spring bulbs certainly gladden the heart of all who see them, whether they are growing in their own gardens or in a bunch bought from a florist, and many of them have a delightful delicacy and charm. Tiny snowdrops often live up to their name by flowering in thick snow, and other small bulbs, such as the pretty *Iris reticulata*, crocuses and scillas brighten up the house or garden. The gardener and writer Vita Sackville-West once suggested digging up a patch of these early spring bulbs just before they come into flower and placing them, with their soil, in a shallow dish so they can be enjoyed in comfort indoors, and it is an idea well worth copying.

My love for blue flowers is certainly catered for each spring, when bulbs bloom in every conceivable shade from palest sky blue to rich cerulean. I love

grape hyacinths (*Muscari*), and you can grow many varieties of these versatile bulbs, including a strange fluffy one called *M. comosum* 'Plumosum'. All the varieties need full sun when growing as shade will encourage them to produce more leaves at the expense of their flowers.

SUCCESSFUL arrangements of flowers often depend as much on your choice of container as the flowers themselves, and the photograph of the *Muscari* on the facing page is a case in point. Gone are the days, luckily, when vases were stiff formal things into which flowers were placed at unnatural angles and seemingly against their will. Containers can now be anything from enamel bowls to teapots, as well as classic vases, and many items that usually nestle forgotten at the back of kitchen cupboards or dining room sideboards can be brought out and used for flower arrangements. Even prettily shaped jam jars can make good vases for a kitchen windowsill, perhaps filled with a mixture of fresh herbs and nasturtiums or a few dog roses straight from the garden. It is good fun and also rewarding to build up a collection of vases and containers for your flowers. Try to include in your collection various shapes, sizes and colours and adapt them to your changing needs. Glass vases are indispensable but try pressed glass, painted porcelain, creamware jugs, old terracotta bowls, baskets and carnival glass bowls.

There should be some reason for putting the container with the flowers: you may have a vase that exactly matches the colouring of a particular flower, or you might want to fill a small blue and white jug with small blue and white flowers. If you choose a vase that completely contrasts with the flowers, make sure it does not overwhelm them – choose a container that echoes and is sympathetic to them. A highly patterned vase may compete with the flowers, producing an ill-matched, complicated and uneasy effect.

GLASS VASES ARE ESPECIALLY BEAUTIFUL CONTAINERS, NOT ONLY BECAUSE OF THEIR LOVELY SHAPES BUT ALSO THEIR SUBTLE COLOURS. YOU CAN BUILD UP YOUR COLLECTION GRADUALLY, HUNTING AROUND ANTIQUE SHOPS AND OTHER PLACES TO FIND UNUSUAL CONTAINERS.

Flat, matt colours work particularly well for vases and are preferable to highly glossed finishes which are too reflective and distract the eye.

As flowers often behave like naughty children they sometimes refuse to face the front of an arrangement, instead twisting their heads away or diving downwards at a dizzying angle. When they insist on doing this there is no point in struggling with them because forcing never works. Books on formal flower arranging discuss such items as floral foam and crumpled chicken wire (leave it for the chickens), which are just two of the devices used to hold flowers in place, but I would not recommend either of them. Having tried chicken wire on several occasions I gave it up as a bad job after becoming frustrated, impatient and tied up in knots. The same goes for string, pin supports and wires – get rid of them if you really want to feel your flowers, because tortured arrangements involving these mechanics will sacrifice the natural beauty of the flowers for clever techniques.

Garden flowers have a more natural, softer flow than florists' flowers, so treat them more tenderly when arranging them and almost allow them to arrange themselves in a vase. I am not advocating the 'bung them in a vase' theory, but you will see from the photographs in this book that I believe flowers should be treated with respect and in ways that bring out their very best.

*I*T is a very pleasant occupation to concoct ways in which to use roses. The Greeks, Romans and Egyptians long ago discovered how to extract the perfume from roses by steeping them in water or oil. They were useful for medicines but came into their own when making perfumes and cosmetics. Rose essential oil is still used today in beauty preparations because of its ability to smooth out the skin, and also for its unforgettable and unmistakable fragrance. Pouring a few drops of rose essential oil into the bath water is a delicious way of relaxing after a long day (you can also add a few drops of lavender or orange essential oils for

THIS IS A CLASSICALLY SIMPLE ARRANGEMENT OF MICHAELMAS DAISIES. THE STARRY CHARM OF THESE DAISY-LIKE FLOWERS IS EMPHASIZED BY THE PLAIN COLOUR AND SHAPE OF THE VASE.

luscious combinations of fragrances), but it can be expensive because you need over ten thousand pounds of rose petals to produce one pound of oil.

A much cheaper alternative has always been rose water, which in the past was not only used in cooking but also as part of the *toilette* and as a room freshener. In the days when water was a precious commodity and hygiene was virtually unheard of, women spent a lot of their time trying to mask the more unpleasant smells that abounded everywhere with lovely floral ones. Rose water was sprinkled on clothes and floors, and pot pourri was placed in bowls in an attempt to keep the air fresh. In Elizabethan times large houses had stillrooms, in which women produced their own potions, lotions and perfumes which were mostly made from roses. This was a very important part of their housekeeping skills and their recipes for pot pourri, pomanders and other perfumed items are still a source of charm and interest today.

I LIKE TO STORE ROSE PETALS IN COLOURED LAYERS IN JARS BECAUSE THEY LOOK SO PRETTY. IT IS ALSO A GOOD WAY OF PREVENTING MY CATS RUMMAGING AROUND IN MY POT POURRI, WHICH THEY LOVE AND TAKE A GREAT INTEREST IN, TOSSING IT HITHER AND THITHER AROUND THE ROOM WHENEVER THEY GET THE CHANCE.

Recollections

THERE'S ROSEMARY, THAT'S FOR REMEMBERANCE; PRAY, LOVE,
REMEMBER; AND THERE IS PANSIES, THAT'S FOR THOUGHTS.

from *Hamlet*, William Shakespeare

PREVIOUS PAGES A BOUQUET
WRAPPED IN RAINBOW CELLOPHANE
INCLUDES SEA LAVENDER
(LIMONIUM), SCABIOUS, EUSTOMA,
SEA HOLLY (ERYNGIUM) AND LILIES.

FACING PAGE ARTICHOKES ARE
VERY ARCHITECTURAL PLANTS AND,
WHEN DRIED, WILL KEEP FOR
MONTHS, DESPITE OFTEN EXPLODING
WITH LARGE SILVER DRIFTS OF
THISTLEDOWN SEEDS.

MEMORIES are often evoked by smells: a whiff of a particular scent can conjure up vivid recollections of days gone by, or even bring back people and places one hasn't thought of in years. Flowers can work in just the same way, for the smell of geraniums instantly makes me think of hot summer afternoons and the fresh rain-soaked scent of narcissi reminds me of those magnificent spring days when the air is like champagne and life seems full of promise.

I wouldn't be without these little cameos from my garden history, which are immediately brought to mind by the scent of flowers. This potent magic can even conjure up visions of places one has never visited — you might be transported to Provence when arranging sunflowers in a jug, imagining their cheerful faces nodding happily in the fields, or the smell of gardenias, orange blossom and jasmine might make you imagine still, starry nights in ancient Greece.

Some flowers are particularly noted for their perfume. Many spring flowers have delicate, elusive scents, such as auriculas, primroses and bluebells. Hyacinths have a rich, obvious perfume which unfortunately can easily become cloying and overpowering (and is even believed by some people to be toxic), while lilies of the valley and violets both have a heavenly fragrance that is made more precious by their brief flowering seasons. Stephanotis, gardenias, stock, honeysuckle and jasmine are all unbeatable plants for their perfume, as are oleander and sweet peas.

What wond'rous life is this I lead!
Ripe applies drop about my head;
The luscious clusters of the vine
Upon my mouth do crush their wine;
The nectarine, and curious peach,
Into my hands themselves do reach;
Stumbling on melons, as I pass,
Insnared with flowers, I fall on grass.

How well the skilful gardener drew
Of flowers, and herbs, this dial new,
Where, from above, the milder sun
Does through a fragrant zodiac run,
And, as it works the industrious bee
Computes its time as well as we!
How could such sweet and wholesome hours
Be reckoned but with herbs and flowers?

from *The Garden*, Andrew Marvell

A SPRIG OF PLUMBAGO AND A SLICE
OF PUMPKIN ARE AN UNLIKELY
COMBINATION BUT HERE THEY
CREATE A SENSE OF TIME PASSING
IN QUIET REFLECTION AND SERENITY.

Roses are among our most fragrant flowers, and the different varieties have different scents. Some have the distinct smell of cold cream, some of honey, some of lemon and moss roses, not content with having scented flowers, also have mossy-smelling foliage. Hold a rose to your nose, drink in its intoxicating fragrance and you will understand why this heavenly flower was thought to have such wide healing powers and be able to soothe and nourish the mind and spirit.

Some plants and flowers keep their fragrance even when dried. Herbs retain their aromatic oils for a long time, of course, and even the smell of shop-bought dried herbs can transport you back to summer gardens. Lavender flowers keep their scent long after their season is over and are excellent ingredients for pot pourri or small lavender-filled bags for hanging in wardrobes. A rose pressed between the pages of a thick book will keep for many years, and its dusty perfume will invade your senses whenever you smell it. I keep many such precious objects, and most of my heavy books are home to cornflowers, pink poinsettia petals, violas and many different leaves, all of which I have tried to save from the treacherous clutches of time.

'SEASON of mists and mellow fruitfulness' is the way the poet John Keats described the autumn, but for me it is also a time for looking back over the year that is so quickly drawing to a close.

Flowers are still valiantly blooming in the garden, with some brave plants producing flowers until the first frosts blacken and wither them, although many more are dying down for the winter. Annuals and biennials, which only flower for one year, are busy putting all their might into producing seed heads that will shoot their contents into the surrounding soil and ensure plenty of seedlings to continue their dynasty come the spring, while herbaceous perennials are dying back so as to conserve their energy during the hard winter months and keep their crowns safe and snug under the soil.

THE MORE BEAUTIFUL THE FLOWER, THE LOVELIER ITS VASE SHOULD BE, AND THESE ELEGANT GLASS VASES ARE THE IDEAL CONTAINERS FOR FRAGILE FLORISTS' ROSES.

MANY SORBUS TREES ARE GROWN
ESPECIALLY FOR THE SHERBERT-
COLOURED BERRIES THEY PRODUCE
IN SUCH GLORIOUS PROFUSION EACH
AUTUMN. THE BERRIES LAST FOR
WEEKS IF THE WATER IN
THEIR CONTAINER IS
CHANGED FREQUENTLY.

Sorbus trees and shrubs are
deciduous and will happily grow
in most situations, although
generally speaking they prefer
moist soils to dry ones. The
berries vary in colour from
white, cream and orange to
flushed pink, scarlet
and deep red.

Of course, the part of the world in which you live
will govern the feeling of autumn for you. In hot
places flowers will bloom again and again with
scarcely a thought for the passing months, while in
others the seasons are marked out by distinct changes
in the weather and in the garden. For the lucky resi-
dents of these areas, autumn is a time when the trees
blaze with red and orange leaves and the setting sun
can look like a huge red ball in a grey sky. This is a
time of year that everyone can enjoy, whether they
are keen gardeners or not. Walking through fallen
leaves in the autumn must surely remind most adults
of their childhoods and the joy of kicking the leaves
about, with the exciting crackling noise when very
dry leaves are trodden underfoot.

As the flowers die back the berries take over in the
autumn, and many shrubs in the gardens and
hedgerows bedeck themselves in glistening fruits that
appeal to humans and birds alike. As well as the
boiled sweet colours of the berries produced by the
sorbus family shown on the facing page, there are the
clusters of shiny red, orange or yellow fruits of pyra-
cantha (but watch out for their thorns) and the juicy
red berries of rowans. The most versatile family of
shrubs and trees must go to the viburnums, however,
many of which not only produce heavenly vanilla-
scented flowers in the spring but then brighten up the
end of the year with their wonderful berries that
range from duck egg blue to deepest black.

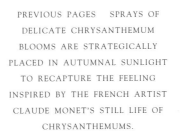

PREVIOUS PAGES   SPRAYS OF
DELICATE CHRYSANTHEMUM
BLOOMS ARE STRATEGICALLY
PLACED IN AUTUMNAL SUNLIGHT
TO RECAPTURE THE FEELING
INSPIRED BY THE FRENCH ARTIST
CLAUDE MONET'S STILL LIFE OF
CHRYSANTHEMUMS.

LEFT   PARROT TULIPS ARE
INDISPENSABLE FLOWERS FOR
CREATING DRAMA, BUT LOOK BEST
WHEN THEY REACH THIS
FLAMBOYANT STAGE, EVOKING
THE MAGNIFICENT DUTCH PAINTINGS
OF THE EIGHTEENTH CENTURY.

HOW I should love to step back in time, to visit ancient streets, peep into windows and, no matter how briefly, become part of another age. I know I could get truly lost in Provins in about 1550, for it was in this French town near Paris that every apothecary's shop was filled with the medicinal rose *Rosa gallica* 'Officinalis'. As a tribute to its history it is still known as the apothecary's rose today and continues to be grown, which is miraculous when you consider it was first taken to France from its natural home in Damascus in the thirteenth century.

Tracing the history of the rose is a fascinating pursuit, although it is only from the eighteenth century that the story really gathers pace. The Romans grew many roses for decoration, and the Cursaders brought damask roses to Europe from the Middle East. The

THE VERDIGRIS GOBLET
COMPLEMENTS THE SOFT, SUGARY
TEXTURE OF THE PETALS OF THESE
'MAESTRO' ROSES, WHICH
NATURALLY LOOK AS THOUGH
THEY HAVE BEEN DUSTED WITH
ICING SUGAR.

rose was highly revered, not only as a magnificent flower but also as a medicine and source of scent. It has also been an emblem of secrecy – the Latin phrase *sub rosa*, meaning 'in confidence', is literally translated as 'under the rose' and refers to the time when secret meetings were held beneath carvings of the flower. The rose has also been mentioned in battles, with the English Wars of the Roses perhaps being the prime example when the Yorkists took the emblem of the white rose and the Lancastrians adopted the red one.

Albas, centifolias, damasks and moss roses were all taken to Europe and cultivated over the succeeding centuries, but it wasn't until the end of the eighteenth century, when repeat-flowering china roses and tea roses were introduced from China, that rose breeders were able to work their magic in real earnest.

I think that anyone who truly loves flowers and has a garden should learn a little about the story of the rose, especially if they want to grow some of the old varieties. To me, roses are particularly exciting because of their history – and also they bear some of the most beautiful flowers in the plant kingdom.

It is customary to choose roses for practical reasons, such as the hardiness and disease resistance of the rugosas, but they could also be chosen for their history. How wonderful to grow the alba rose 'Great Maiden's Blush' (if you prefer, you can use its bewitching French names of 'Cuisse de Nymphe' or 'La Seduisante'), knowing that it was painted by the

Favourite roses can be dried by carefully burying them in powdered silica crystals but I find leaving them in a warm airy room or cupboard is the best method to use. It seems gentler and better preserves the fragile character of the flowers.

RECOLLECTIONS

HYBRID TEA ROSES TAKEN STRAIGHT
FROM THE GARDEN LOOK AT THEIR
MOST BEAUTIFUL WHILE WAITING TO
BE ARRANGED. A GENEROUS
HANDFUL OF ROSE PETALS
SPRINKLED INTO A BOWL OF FRESH
JASMINE BLOSSOM MAKES AN
INSTANT BUT RAVISHING
POT POURRI.

PREVIOUS PAGES A SOFT MIXTURE
CAPTURES THE MOOD OF A PERFECT
SUMMER'S DAY. THE FLOWERS
INCLUDE THE CLEMATIS 'VYVYAN
PENNELL', ORIENTAL POPPIES,
SCABIOUS, PEONIES, PANSIES AND
THE ROSE 'GERTRUDE JEKYLL'.

BELOW THE DELICATE DANDELION
SEEDHEADS CONTRAST WITH THE
BOLD SINGLE CRIMSON GLORY VINE
(VITIS COIGNETIAE) LEAF. THE
LEAVES OF THIS ORNAMENTAL
PLANT RETAIN THEIR DRAMATIC
GREEN AND RED COLOURING
EVEN WHEN DRIED.

great French artist Redoute, or 'Marie Louise', a damask raised in the Empress Josephine's famous garden at Malmaison in 1813. There are also roses to be grown for their prolonged flowering season, such as the ancient rose 'Old Blush China', which can flower for seven months non-stop. The attractive rosehips that are borne when the flowers are spent are another consideration, for they range through every shade of red and orange and all sorts of shapes.

It is a great pleasure to look at photographs of roses and mentally compile lists of all the ones you

THIS GREEN GLASS CONTAINER
IS FILLED WITH FLORISTS' ROSES,
WHICH ASSUME A SOFT PAPERY
LOOK AND CRUMPLE INWARDS WHEN
THEY BEGIN TO FADE.

covet, but you should also visit some of the gardens and nurseries that are so rightly famed for them, so you can observe them at close quarters.

If you don't have a garden but love roses, you will find florists' roses very different from the ones grown in gardens. They have much straighter stems and tidier flowers, and so create quite formal arrangements.

FLOWERS have always been a perfect way to celebrate a special occasion or simply to remind someone that you are thinking of them, but your kind thought will lose its meaning if you don't choose flowers that are appropriate. There is little point in

Many weeds are very pretty, which proves that one man's weed is another man's flower. Jars and jugs of them look lovely on windowsills, especially when arranged in informal or higgledy-piggledy groups.

A FAVOURITE PAINTING MAY INSPIRE
YOU TO CREATE A MIRROR IMAGE
WITH FLOWERS. HERE, THE
CYMBIDIUM ORCHID IN THE BOTTLE
ECHOES THE PAINTING WITH ITS
CHEQUERED BOARD AND BOTTLE,
MAKING A CONFUSION OF REALITY.
WHERE DOES REAL LIFE BEGIN AND
THE PAINTING END?

sending orange gerberas to someone who loathes the colour, or strong-smelling narcissi to a chronic hay-fever sufferer. Without wishing to be sexist, men tend to like rather robust flowers, and some men are so wary of being given flowers (or so they will have you believe) that you might be best choosing flowers that are quite masculine, such as proteas, alliums or sunflowers. To continue the theme, you could wrap the blooms in black tissue paper, or plain brown paper, tied with thin brown velvet ribbon or raffia. If you wish to use tissue paper, you will first have to wrap the wet flower stems in cling film to prevent any moisture seeping through the paper and ruining it.

For a more flamboyant friend, layers of different colours of tissue paper, with each one visible, can be wrapped around a bouquet of flowers that might include a dazzling mixture of 'Stargazer' lilies, glory lilies (*Gloriosa superba* 'Rothschildiana') and a few stems of *Cattleya* orchids.

In the photograph on pages 98–99 I used rainbow cellophane which is a marvellous wrapping for flowers because it catches the light beautifully and also gives the blooms some protection while in transit from giver to recipient. Use it lavishly and secure it with a huge velvet or paper bow.

If you want understatement, wrap a wide piece of lace around a bunch of flowers, then tie it firmly with satin or velvet ribbon. The Elizabethans used to give posies, called tussy-mussies, which included every-

PREVIOUS PAGES KOHLRABI AND
FENNEL SIT SIDE BY SIDE, IDEAL
COMPANIONS FOR AN ARRANGEMENT
THAT EVOKES THE FEEL OF
THE COUNTRYSIDE.

RIGHT THIS SIMPLE AUTUMNAL
STILL LIFE SHOWS JUST HOW
BEAUTIFUL BUDDLEIA CAN BE WHEN
USED AS A CUT FLOWER. IT LASTS
VERY WELL IN WATER AND IS A
WELCOME ADDITION TO THE MORE
USUAL REPERTOIRE OF
AUTUMN FLOWERS.

Buddleia is a persistent, hardy
shrub that happily forces itself
through chinks in walls and
merrily grows on derelict land
and along railway tracks.
Butterflies adore its flowers and
great numbers of them can be
seen fluttering in playful
worship over this attractive
plant.

thing from their gardens and hedgerows, from leaves, herbs and twigs to seed heads, grasses and flowers. If you wanted to use old-fashioned plants you could choose from roses, pinks (which the Elizabethans called gilly flowers), rosemary, cornflowers, lavender, mint, summer snowflakes (*Leucojum*), Jacob's ladder (*Polemonium caeruleum*) or aquilegia to create a posy that would surely gladden the heart.

Tied posies are very beautiful. Gather the flowers in your hand, putting them in the position they will have in their container, until you are happy with the posy. Tie the ends of the stalks together firmly with raffia or garden twine, then trim the ends of the stalks to the same length and wrap the posy in cellophane or just tie with some lovely ribbon. Your gift will be remembered long after the flowers are gone.

CARING FOR FLOWERS

As soon as a flower has been cut from its parent plant the length of its survival is determined by the way it is treated, so you must try to reproduce its natural environment as much as possible.

Once a flower has been cut it is prone to attack from bacteria which multiply rapidly in water and which can enter its stem, thereby reducing its ability to take up water. Some flowers, and especially roses, are notorious for drooping heads or buds which fail to open in water — both problems which are frequently caused by bacteria blocking their stems. You can help to combat this problem by always using scrupulously clean containers, removing all leaves below the water level and adding a little flower food to the water. These special preparations contain a mild disinfectant to inhibit the bacteria and a sugar, such as saccharose or glucose, which feeds the flowers and encourages all the buds to open. Flower food also means you don't have to change the water, although vases may need topping up during hot weather or if the flowers are very thirsty. Old-fashioned remedies involving white wine or lemonade and a drop of bleach do work but should only be used in emergencies, as it is crucial to use the right balance of ingredients. Commercially-produced flower food gives more consistent results and is more economical to use.

Another common reason for drooping flowers is stem tips that have dried out. You can avoid this by always cutting off the end of each stem diagonally with a knife, thereby maximizing the surface area of the stem and increasing the intake of water. Contrary to popular belief, stems should never be smashed, not even the woodiest ones, because extensive research has proved that a crushed stem is very prone to bacterial infection and its damaged fibres are less efficient in taking up water.

Flowers cut from the garden appreciate several hours' of conditioning in a deep container of fresh cold water, before being arranged. Florists' flowers should already have been treated this way in the shop, but their stems should be cut again if they have been out of water for more than an hour.

When selecting flowers, whether from the garden or a florist, always choose blooms that are not fully developed (with the possible exception of dahlias). Avoid flowers with weak, droopy stems and petals or discoloured leaves, don't place them in direct sunlight and, if you are transporting them, keep them well wrapped up and if possible ensure the the ends of the stems are in water or surrounded by damp paper. If you want to cut flowers from the garden, do so in the morning before the sun has become too hot, and place the flowers in water as soon as possible. Leaving a bunch of flowers on the grass while you hunt around the garden for more treasures will dry them out very quickly and, on a very hot day, could even kill them altogether.

The life of cut flowers varies according to the species, but you will get the best out of them if you avoid leaving them in full sun, extremes of temperature and draughts. Placing flowers near ripening fruit also ages them prematurely because they are affected by the ethylene gas produced by all ageing plants.

Some people swear by keeping flowers in a refrigerator to prolong their lives, but it can actually be harmful because domestic refrigerators do not provide humidity. The fridge can be used in an emergency, providing the stems are placed in water and the flowers wrapped in a plastic bag to conserve their moisture, but a far better remedy is to keep the flowers in deep water in a cool, dark room.

You can prolong the life of flowers still further by snipping off faded blooms and checking the water level regularly. Remove any flowers that have died, rearrange the remaining ones and cut down their stems drastically, removing all the foliage (which often dies before the flowers themselves).

USEFUL TIPS FOR INDIVIDUAL FLOWERS
The following tips are most appropriate for commercially-grown flowers, as these are produced specifically for cutting and bred for longevity. However, the basic principles apply whether the flowers have been grown in a garden or bought from a florist.

Alstroemeria These flowers are available virtually all year round and their popularity is largely due to the abundance of flower heads and their impressive longevity — they will keep for three to four weeks in a constant cool temperature.

Anemone Always buy anemones in coloured bud. If the ends have dried out, wrap the stems in paper to keep them straight and give them a drink in deep water. Anemones open very quickly and last for between eight and twelve days.

Amaryllis Choose flowers with three or four fat buds and with one nearly or fully open. If you use cut flower food designed for bulb flowers, the amaryllis should last for at least two weeks. The ends of the stems tend to splay out when standing in water, but this can be avoided by wrapping a piece of clear adhesive tape around the end of each stem. A fully mature flower head is very heavy, so inserting a thin stick inside the stem will give support and prevent the flower keeling over.

Chrysanthemum Modern hybrids can last for a month or so, although the foliage usually dies before the blooms. Chrysanthemums emit a large amount of ethylene gas so are better kept apart from ethylene-sensitive flowers like carnations, antirrhinums and orchids, unless the room temperature is quite cool.

Dahlia Unlike other flowers, dahlias should be cut or bought when they are fully open. Be particularly vigilant about removing all leaves which may touch the vase water. Dahlias last for between six and fourteen days.

Delphinium (Larkspur) The tallest varieties have hollow stems which can be filled with water and plugged with a little cotton wool to prolong their lives. Commercially-grown delphiniums are often specially treated to stop the petals shedding, and these flowers last for about ten to twelve days.

Dianthus (Carnation, Garden Pink) These flowers are long-lasting but very sensitive to ethylene. This tendency can be reduced by using cut flower food specially designed for carnations.

Freesias The upper buds of these flowers will continue to open if the lower faded blooms are snipped off. The flowers like sugar added' to the vase water and, if kept cool, will last for about two weeks.

Gerbera These flowers are very prone to bacteria, so you must ensure the containers are perfectly clean and cut flower food is always used. If the stems become limp, place the flowers in a tall container with water right up to their necks until the stems straighten again. If looked after carefully gerberas will last for about three weeks.

Hyacinth Choose stems where the first flowers of the raceme are open. Always use cut flower food designed for bulbs. Cut off any roots but leave the dark part of the stem intact as this is the food reservoir and ensures longevity. They should last between twelve and sixteen days if kept cool and misted regularly.

Lily Most varieties last for at least two weeks. Cut off the lower blooms as they fade and encourage the upper buds to open by gently teasing out their petals.

Narcissus (Daffodil) All the narcissus family emit a latex from their stems when cut, which is known as 'daffodil slime' and is harmful to other flowers. Either keep the daffodils separate or use the special cut flower food that makes them safe to mix with other flowers. Daffodils last for about a week, but if bought in tight green bud there will be extra days as the flowers mature and open.

Orchid Many of these delicate flowers are sold in vials of treated water and their stems should never be allowed to dry out. Orchids will last for at least a month if kept cool and frequently misted. If they become limp they should be immersed in water for at least an hour. Orchids are very susceptible to ethylene gas so should be kept away from ripening fruit, vegetables and decaying flowers.

Roses Most roses should last for between eight to eighteen days, depending on the variety and room temperature. One clean diagonal cut at the end of each stem improves longevity, as does standing the roses in deep, lukewarm water for several hours before arranging them. Removing thorns will provide entrance holes for bacteria, although it is advisable if the roses are being arranged for a hand-held posy. Frequent misting keeps both the blooms and the leaves fresh.

Tulips Removing the lower white part of the stem will improve longevity. Tulips continue growing in water — anything up to 5 cm (2 in) in the first couple of days — but this can be avoided by using distilled water and omitting any flower food. They will curve towards the light and if the stems are bent this can be rectified by wrapping them tightly in wet paper and standing them in deep water with the light directly above them.

Woody stems Branches of blossom (*Prunus*), lilac (*Syringa*) or guelder roses (*Viburnum*) make bold dramatic arrangements and last extremely well if treated with their own special cut flower food. Do not crush or hammer the stems, but make a clean cut using a sharp knife or, if the branch is too thick, with a pair of secateurs.

The Flowers & Plants Association

INDEX